The **Essential** Buyer's Guide

BMW
GS

1980-2007

Your marque expert:
Peter Henshaw

VELOCE PUBLISHING
THE PUBLISHER OF FINE AUTOMOTIVE BOOKS

Also from Veloce Publishing –

Essential Buyer's Guide Series
Alfa GT (Booker)
Alfa Romeo Spider Giulia (Booker & Talbott)
Audi TT (Davies)
Austin Seven (Barker)
Big Healeys (Trummel)
BMW E21 3 Series (1975-1983) (Reverente, Cook)
BMW GS (Henshaw)
BMW X5 (Saunders)
BSA 500 & 650 Twins (Henshaw)
BSA Bantam (Henshaw)
Citroën 2CV (Paxton)
Citroën ID & DS (Heilig)
Cobra Replicas (Ayre)
Corvette C2 Sting Ray 1963-1967 (Falconer)
Ducati Bevel Twins (Falloon)
Ducati Desmodue Twins (Falloon)
Ducati Desmoquattro Twins (Falloon)
Fiat 500 & 600 (Bobbitt)
Ford Capri (Paxton)
Ford Escort Mk1 & Mk2 (Williamson)
Ford Mustang (Cook)
Ford RS Cosworth Sierra & Escort (Williamson)
Harley-Davidson Big Twins (Henshaw)
Hinckley Triumph triples & fours 750, 900, 955, 1000, 1050, 1200 – 1991-2009 (Henshaw)
Honda CBR600 Hurricane (Henshaw)
Honda CBR FireBlade (Henshaw)
Honda SOHC fours 1969-1984 (Henshaw)
Jaguar E-type 3.8 & 4.2-litre (Crespin)
Jaguar E-type V12 5.3-litre (Crespin)
Jaguar XJ 1995-2003 (Crespin)
Jaguar XK8 & XKR (1996-2005) (Thorley)
Jaguar/Daimler XJ6, XJ12 & Sovereign (Crespin)
Jaguar/Daimler XJ40 (Crespin)
Jaguar Mark 1 & 2 (All models including Daimler 2.5-litre V8) 1955 to 1969 (Thorley)
Jaguar S-type – 1999 to 2007 (Thorley)
Jaguar X-type – 2001 to 2009 (Thorley)
Jaguar XJ-S (Crespin)
Jaugar XJ6, XJ8 & XJR (Thorley)
Jaguar XK 120, 140 & 150 (Thorley)

Kawasaki Z1 & Z900 (Orritt)
Land Rover Series I, II & IIA (Thurman)
Land Rover Series III (Thurman)
Lotus Seven replicas & Caterham 7: 1973-2013 (Hawkins)
Mazda MX-5 Miata (Mk1 1989-97 & Mk2 98-2001) (Crook)
Mercedes-Benz 280SL-560DSL Roadsters (Bass)
Mercedes-Benz 'Pagoda' 230SL, 250SL & 280SL (Bass)
MGA 1955-1962 (Sear, Crosier)
MGF & MG TF (Hawkins)
MGB & MGB GT (Williams)
MG Midget & A-H Sprite (Horler)
MG TD, TF & TF1500 (Jones)
Mini (Paxton)
Morris Minor & 1000 (Newell)
New Mini (Collins)
Norton Commando (Henshaw)
Peugeot 205 GTI (Blackburn)
Porsche 911 (930) Turbo series (Streather)
Porsche 911 (964) (Streather)
Porsche 911 (993) (Streather)
Porsche 911 (996) (Streather)
Porsche 911 Carrera 3.2 series 1984 to 1989 (Streather)
Porsche 911SC – Coupé, Targa, Cabriolet & RS Model years 1978-1983 (Streather)
Porsche 924 – All models 1976 to 1988 (Hodgkins)
Porsche 928 (Hemmings)
Porsche 930 Turbo & 911 (930) Turbo (Streather)
Porsche 944 (Higgins, Mitchell)
Porsche 986 Boxster series (Streather)
Porsche 987 Boxster and Cayman series (Streather)
Rolls-Royce Silver Shadow & Bentley T-Series (Bobbitt)
Subaru Impreza (Hobbs)
Triumph Bonneville (Henshaw)
Triumph Stag (Mort & Fox)
Triumph TR7 & TR8 (Williams)
Triumph Thunderbird, Trophy & Tiger (Henshaw)
Vespa Scooters – Classic two-stroke models 1960-2008 (Paxton)
Volvo 700/900 Series (Beavis)
VW Beetle (Cservenka & Copping)
VW Bus (Cservenka & Copping)
VW Golf GTI (Cservenka & Copping)

www.veloce.co.uk

For post publication news, updates and amendments relating to this book please visit www.veloce.co.uk/books/V4135

Animals and everything related to them!
www.hubbleandhattie.com

BATTLE CRY!
Books that explore any and every facet of military history
www.battlecry-books.com

First published in February 2008 and reprinted in January 2014 by Veloce Publishing Limited, Veloce House, Parkway Farm Business Park, Middle Farm Way, Poundbury, Dorchester, Dorset, DT1 3AR, England.
Fax 01305 250479/e-mail info@veloce.co.uk/web www.veloce.co.uk or www.velocebooks.com.

ISBN: 978-1-84584-135-5 UPC: 636847041359

If you've always fancied a BMW, but thought you couldn't live with the touring image, then a GS could change all that. This book aims to show the good and bad points of GS ownership, and what to look for when buying one secondhand. There are plenty of them out there, and despite BMW's upmarket image, the GS can be a quite affordable bike to run. Examples also hold their value well, so while buying one might seem like a big investment, you should lose less in depreciation than with other bikes.

An ageing R80 GS can still give years of service.

The original G/S (it stood for 'Gelande/Strasse' – Off-road/Street) made a huge impact when it was launched back in 1980. It pioneered the concept of a large trail bike that could comfortably be used on the road, and proved to be a winning formula, with thousands sold over the next quarter century. Although most were bought by road riders, the GS also became the bike of choice for overland travellers, in whose hands these bikes have explored every part of the globe. In fact, so successful was

Latest R1200 GS is a comfortable and sophisticated machine.

the GS concept that just about every major motorcycle manufacturer has since launched an 'adventure sport' bike to suit.

That first G/S was updated as the R80 GS in 1988, alongside the one-litre R100, before the all-new oilhead (as in oil-cooled) R1100 GS in 1993. The old-generation 'airheads' carried on for a while, but the 1100 grew into the 1150, then the 1200 GS, with the optioned-up Adventure models for those who really did want to take one off-road, or look as if they might.

In its 25 years of production, the BMW GS has become a milestone bike, fully deserving its tag of the 'two-wheeled Range Rover'. Just like drivers of that eponymous 4x4, most owners will never take their GS off-road, but like the image that goes with it, not to mention the side benefits of comfortable, long-travel suspension and fine ground clearance. In 2004, Ewan McGregor and Charley Boorman's Long Way Round proved that the BMW GS could walk the walk as well. Buy one, and you won't just be owning a practical, comfortable, long-lived bike, but there's the suggestion that you could – if you felt like it – head off across the Sahara tomorrow.

Acknowledgements

Thanks go to all those people who helped, and without whom this book would not have happened. Dave Wyndham and staff at CW Motorcycles (www.cwmotorcycles. co.uk, 01305 269370) allowed me to photograph various GSs, and provided lots of useful information on oilheads. Phil Hawksley (the Boxer Man, www.boxerman. co.uk, 0116 266 8913) also gave his time and in-depth knowledge of airheads. Thanks go to overland traveller Sam Manicom (I can recommend his book, *Under Asian Skies*) and to Les Madge of Travel-Dri Plus for giving me their bikes to photograph. Also to Ted Simon, who rode a friend's R100 GS around the world in 2001, reliving his original 1970s trip, at the age of 72. Finally, I'm grateful to any other owners whose bikes appear in this book, but whom I wasn't able to track down!

Some GSs lead adventurous lives!

Essential Buyer's Guide™ currency

At the time of publication a BG unit of currency "●" equals approximately £1.00/ US$1.60/Euro 1.20. Please adjust to suit current exchange rates.

Contents

Tall and short riders

If you're below average height, make sure you have a good ride on a GS before committing to buying one. These are tall, heavy bikes that aren't kind to short legs – later GSs have a height-adjustable seat, but the choice is between tall and very tall. On the other hand, they suit six-footers very well.

Running costs

Surprisingly modest, as long as you don't need to buy many spares. Servicing is every 6000 miles and the oilheads can manage 50mpg. Airheads are less frugal – 45-50mpg for the Monolever, 40-45 for the Paralever.

Maintenance

No chain to adjust or lube, reasonable tyre life, and those 6000-mile service intervals are relatively far apart for a bike. There's also very little brightwork to keep shiny on a GS, though it does benefit from having any road salt off washed off.

Usability

With the proviso above about weight and seat height, the GS is a thoroughly usable day-to-day, all year round sort of bike. It's very comfortable, with a relaxed, upright riding position, and usually comes with decent luggage.

Parts availability

Excellent. BMW offers spares for all airheads and oilheads, and there's also a whole community of BMW specialists (often cheaper) who know the bikes inside out and offer good alternatives to genuine BMW spares.

A GS can make a reliable all-year-round motorcycle.

Parts costs

Not too bad. The parts costs quoted in Chapter 2 are from an independent specialist. Dealer prices will be higher, but in general parts seem no more expensive than for the equivalent Japanese machine.

Insurance group

These are big bikes, expensive to repair after a prang, so insurance isn't the cheapest, but the 1100 and 1150GS are a reasonable Group 13, and the airheads Group 9. The older airheads may be eligible for cheaper classic limited-mileage policies.

Investment potential

Not much. The GS has always been a big seller – at the time of writing it was BMW's best selling model, and had been for some time – so there's little rarity value. Original Paris Dakar bikes will surely be collectable in the future.

Foibles

The GS is a quirky bike – no other manufacturer (Ural apart) uses this engine layout, Telelever front end or Paralever rear. And it looks like nothing else on the road. Telelever feels different to the conventional forks that most of us are used to, and the gearchange on early bikes is an acquired taste.

Plus points

Shaft drive; the odd suspension works very well; the 'torquey' reliable engine can do high mileage with little more than routine maintenance; all-day comfort. Plenty of plus points, then.

Minus points

The GS may be just too quirky for some, too big and heavy for others. The older airheads are thirsty and no bike this big will ever be cheap to run.

Alternatives

Plenty – the GS pioneered the adventure tourer sector, but countless competitors have followed in its wake. Honda Varadero, Triumph Tiger, Suzuki V-Strom, Ducati Multistrada, KTM Adventure, Aprilia Caponord and, at a pinch, the Yamaha TDM.

2 Cost considerations
– affordable, or a money pit?

Brembo brake calipers are easy to find.

Parts are surprisingly affordable, though you will save money by buying from an independent specialist rather than a BMW dealer – the prices quoted here are from an independent. It's the same for servicing (though not everyone has an independent nearby). Paralever airheads are heavy on fuel.

R80/100GS
Front disc x85 (OE, 184)
Front brake pads x18.74
Clutch plate x51.70
Wiring loom (R80 G/S) x115
Gasket set x52
Piston (R100GS) x81
Exhaust system (Keihan s/s) x340
Rear shock (OE) x203
Rear shock (Ohlins) x480
Air filter element x17
Oil filter element x7.76
Front tyre (Continental Twinduro) x59
Rear tyre (Continental Twinduro) x78

R1100/1150GS
Front disc x99 (OE, 132)
Brake caliper repair kit x40
Speedo cable x14.50

Clutch (complete) x195
Starter motor x182
Exhaust valve x69
Silencer (Remus, titanium) x375
Headlight/oil cooler mounting x80
Fuel pump x151
Heated grips x103
Screen (1150) x56
Rear shock (Hagon) x248

R1200GS
Front tyre x74
Oil filter x8.58
Front shock (Ohlins) x435

BMW still supplies parts for all GSs.

BMW dealers, or independent specialists, are good sources for parts.

Servicing
R80/100GS (Independent specialist)
Minor – R80 x106; R100 x113
Major – R80 x204; R100 x 207

R1100/1150/1200GS (BMW dealer)
6000 miles x220
12,000 miles x270,
24,000 miles x320.
If low mileage, there's just an annual
service of fluid/oil changes:
Bikes without EVO ABS braking x160
Bikes with EVO ABS braking x300

Will you get along?

The good news is that the BMW GS is very easy to live with, and the even better news is that this applies to all of them. A 25-year-old R80 G/S will make a tough, everyday workhorse, despite its near-classic status – there are plenty of Japanese and Italian classic bikes of the same age that you couldn't say that of. At the other extreme, a nearly-new R1200 GS might seem like a Sunday toy, but it's just as capable of standing up to high mileages.

GSs make great long distance bikes: the long travel suspension and 'torquey' flat-twin makes them relaxed tourers, worlds away from the often frenetic realm of four cylinders, and it's easy to see why many riders, who have no interest in venturing off-road, buy them as such.

Oilhead GSs, especially the 1150 and 1200, are quite quick bikes – not up to sports bike standards in a straight line, but certainly fast enough for most riders. By contrast the R80 and 100 are a little sluggish by modern standards, though still fast enough to keep up with modern traffic. The oilheads also handle very well indeed, and it's an article of faith among some owners that they can keep up with sports bikes on twisty roads. A combination of grippy tyres, excellent ground clearance and the anti-dive properties of the Telelever front end do the business.

By motorcycle standards, BMW's adventure tourer doesn't require a great deal of maintenance either. Servicing intervals are relatively relaxed (every 6000 miles for oilheads) and the shaft drive means there's no chain to lubricate, adjust or worry about. When the bike does need attention, there's a good community of owners out there, with a whole generation of experience to draw on. In the UK alone, there are two clubs (the long-established BMW Owners Club and the more recent BM Riders Club) plus internet-based clubs specific to the GS – www.ukgser.com and www.gsclubuk.org. There's also a good sprinkling of highly knowledgeable independent specialists, who are invariably long-standing BMW owners themselves. Official BMW dealers may not have the cheapest labour rates (thanks to their overheads) but they generally give excellent service.

BMW GSs are tough and long-lived. Fifty-thousand miles is a relatively high mileage for many motorcycles, but a 50,000-mile GS is in its prime. These bikes take 10-20,000 miles to fully run-in, and standing out in today's throwaway society, they are built to last. Clutches for example (though this depends on rider abuse) should last 50,000 miles on oilheads, longer still on airheads. There are plenty of GSs running around having covered 100,000 miles or more, with the odd 200,000-mile bike cropping up now and then. In short, if you want a bike that will take you to work every day, all year round, and load up with pillion and luggage for a high-mileage European tour come the summer, then here it is.

There must be a downside to all of this, and there is. BMW GSs are big, tall, heavy machines, awkward for shorter riders to manoeuvre. Even the early R80 G/S weighed 186kg, and an 1150 GS (the heaviest of the lot) tips the scales at close to a quarter of a tonne with a full tank of fuel on board. This weight is compounded by a high seat height. The long travel suspension, and extra ground clearance for off-road use, leaves the GS with a seat height of around 850mm or more – that's about two inches higher than a conventional tourer, which doesn't sound much but can mean the difference between having a foot flat and secure on the ground, or flailing around on tiptoes. Oilheads do have an adjustable seat, but there's still no genuinely low seat option, and the Adventures have a higher seat still. Of course, many of these comments could be applied to most of the adventure tourers, and some shorter riders aren't in the least bothered by controlling a big bike – coping with it is more down to confidence and technique rather than strength. On the other hand, anyone can get caught out by a bad camber, and if you're under 5ft 8in or so, check on the test ride that you are comfortable with the GS's size. If an 1100 or 1150 feels too large, consider whether you can afford a 1200, which is usefully lighter and slimmer.

Shaft drive makes the GS easy to live with.

The upside is that this very size makes the BMW an ideal bike for six-footers, who might feel cramped on something smaller.

At the moment, the cheapest BMW GSs are the old generation of airheads, though it's a good bet that original Paris Dakar machines will eventually catch or even overtake oilhead values. That makes an early 80 G/S or 100 GS good value, but there are a few caveats. Braking, especially on the G/S, simply isn't up to modern standards. They're

GSs are big, heavy bikes – will you be comfortable with that?

adequate for modern traffic, but no more, and the bikes need to be ridden with this in mind. The same goes for the gearchange: notchy and noisy on the G/S, though it did improve over the years, and later oilheads are far better in this respect.

By classic bike standards, airhead GSs are relatively modern, but many are now over 20 years old, and the wiring and electrical components may be ready to give trouble. There's one more thing about the airheads – they are relatively thirsty, especially the R100, which returns 40-45mpg, so even if you don't have to spend much on everyday maintenance, the fuel bill could be high. Oilheads, unless thrashed, are far more efficient. They also, especially the 1200s, pack a lot of electronics – these are pretty reliable, but if anything does go wrong, putting it right is a dealer job. If you like the sort of bike you can fettle, and repair by the roadside, go for an airhead.

Whichever GS you choose, it's likely to be an easy to live with companion, one of those bikes that could tempt you to sell the car and live the two-wheel life all year round.

4 Relative values
– which model for you?

See Chapter 12 for value assessment. This chapter shows, in percentage terms, the relative value of individual models in good condition. It also looks at the strengths and weaknesses of each model, so that you can decide which is best for you. Basically, the GS's evolution can be divided into 'airheads' and 'oilheads', and they are referred to as such throughout this book – they share nothing except the basic layout. Airheads were the air-cooled R80 and R100 and oilheads the new generation of oil-cooled flat-twins built from 1993 onwards. Airheads also divide into the R80 G/S 'Monolever' and R80/100 GS 'Paralever' (1988 on), which refers to the rear suspension/driveshaft arrangement. All oilheads used the Paralever rear end.

Models

Airheads		Oilheads	
R80 G/S	1980-87	R1100GS	1993-99
R80 ST	1982-85	R850GS	1996-2001
R80 & 100GS	1988-96	R1150GS	1998-2004
R80/100 Paris Dakar	1984-94	R1150GS Adventure	2001-06
R80 GS Basic	1996	R1200GS	2004 on
R80 GS Kalahari	1997	R1200GS Adventure	2006 on

R80 G/S 1980-87

The original G/S, which stood for 'Gelande/Strasse' (literally, 'off-road/street') was launched in autumn 1980 as a new breed of large off-road bike that was comfortable on tarmac as well. It made use of BMW's well-proven 797cc flat-twin, in 50bhp form with electronic ignition and voltage regulator, but the all-new feature was the Monolever rear end, using a single-sided swing arm enclosing the driveshaft, and single rear shock. This saved a lot of weight, as did aluminium cylinders and a single-plate diaphragm clutch, though the complete bike still tipped the scales at 186kg, a lot for an off-road bike in those days. Not that the press was put off, and the G/S

Not many early G/Ss are still in original condition.

enjoyed instant acclaim – it was accepted as a great road bike which could take to the rough stuff as well. To complete the transformation of R80 road bike into the dual-purpose G/S came longer travel suspension, a 19.5 litre fuel tank, 21in front wheel, two-into-one exhaust and high-mounted plastic front mudguard, though there were plenty of other detail differences.

Nearly 22,000 G/Ss were sold, though they rarely come up for sale today – you'll be even less likely to find one in original condition, as owners like to accessorize them with big fuel tanks and luggage. Of all the GSs, the original is the least suitable for modern traffic. As a 50bhp 800, it was acceptably quick in 1980, but will feel a little lethargic for anyone used to a modern big bike. The brakes – a 260mm single front disc and 200mm rear drum are best described as adequate, but no more. The controls are heavier than on modern bikes, the gearchange is slower, and the shaft drive reaction lifts the rear end on acceleration. In short, the original R80 G/S is a quarter-century old now, and feels it. But it is lighter than later airheads and its simpler Monolever rear end is less prone to failure.

There were two variations on the G/S. Launched in 1982, the R80 ST was a pure road going version, with a 19in front wheel, reduced suspension travel and a smaller fuel tank, but retaining the Monolever rear end, high-level exhaust and tall chassis. The ST was reckoned to be a slim and nimble bike, with its own appeal, but retained the G/S's high seat; it wasn't a great success, and lasted only three years. More enduring was the Paris Dakar version of the G/S, launched in 1984 to capitalise on BMW's success in the desert rally of the same name. This came with a monster 32-litre fuel tank, Paris Dakar graphics and a solo seat. Because relatively few were made, these Paris Dakars fetch high prices now, though the parts were also available to retro-fit on standard G/Ss.

80%

R80 & 100GS 1988-96
R100 Paris Dakar 1990-94

Original Paris Dakars could become collectors' items.

The second generation GS was launched in autumn 1987, and although it looked similar to the old one, just about everything was new or changed. The frame was reinforced, and the front forks (now from Marzocchi) were wider and longer travel than before. Cross-spoke wheels (which BMW patented) were stronger, and allowed the use of tubeless tyres. The 80 GS (it lost the '/') was joined by the R100 GS, offering 60bhp from its detuned one-litre flat-twin, and 56lb/ft at 3750rpm, plus a standard oil cooler. There was slightly improved braking (from a 285mm front disc, the rear drum was unchanged), a better starter motor, beefier battery and bigger 26-litre fuel tank. But the most significant change was the Paralever rear end, and the new GS was the first BMW so fitted. Adding a second flexible U-joint to the driveshaft, and a strut from the bottom of the final drive to the transmission cancelled out most of the shaft drive reaction on acceleration, and is still used on BMWs today.

A second generation 80 or 100 GS makes a good secondhand buy, combining the essential simplicity of the original with improved dynamics from the Paralever

Some older GSs may be very well-travelled!

Ted Simon's borrowed R80 GS, back from travelling around the world.

rear end. The braking still isn't up to modern standards, though it's better, and the R100 offers useful extra performance, especially when travelling two-up with luggage.

These later airheads are also easier to find than the originals, and over 45,000 were built. If there's a downside, it's that many of the same comments about the road riding experience apply, with performance, braking and handling all below modern standards. The 80/100 GS are also heavy (210kg for the R100) and thirsty (40-45mpg).

Variants include a resurrected Paris Dakar from 1990, based on the R100 GS with a new nose fairing and crashbars. And the R80GS Basic, offered for 1996 only as a run-out model with a smaller 19-litre tank – a rare bike, it's thought that only 3000 were made. Even rarer is the R65 GS, built between 1987 and 1992 and sold in the German market (some also went to Denmark) in 27bhp or 50bhp form. Not much lighter than the R80 GS, and with a lot less power, though with a lower insurance group and rarity value on its side.

R80 GS: 48%
R100 GS: 52%

In 1993, the R1100 heralded a new generation of GS.

R1100 GS – 1993-99

The first new generation oilhead GS represented a complete break with the past, though BMW stuck with the flat-twin engine layout and shaft drive. First off, the all-new oil-cooled flat-twin had four valves per cylinder, high

Rare R850 has no weight advantage over the 1100.

camshaft control and Motronic fuel injection. Despite being detuned, compared to the pure road R1100 RS, with 80bhp and 72lb/ft, the new GS offered far greater performance than the old one, with a six-speed transmission giving relaxed high speed cruising as well. The bike was festooned with electronics, including engine management and the options of a catalytic converter and ABS – the latter could be switched off if the rider so wished. The Paralever rear end was carried over, though now with remote hydraulic adjustment of the spring pre-load. At the front, conventional forks were abandoned in favour of BMW's new Telelever system: two fork sliders carried the front wheel, but the actual suspension was provided by a single spring/damper unit mounted on a substantial A-frame casting. It was an excellent system, more rigid than conventional forks and with some built-in anti-dive characteristics.

For modern traffic conditions, R1100 GS is a whole new ball game. It's a lot faster than the old R100, able to cover huge distances two-up, and very comfortable with it. Nearly 40,000 were sold, as many riders twigged that here was an excellent tourer, even if they never intended to take it off-road. It opened up a whole new market, significantly including riders who would never have otherwise bought a BMW. As icing on the cake, the fuel injection made it far more efficient than the R100, at 50-55mpg, which meant a potential range of over 250 miles.

As a secondhand buy, the R1100 has much going for it. It represents the cheapest route into oilhead GS ownership, and makes for a fast, comfortable tourer, practical to use all year round. The electronics might be complex, but they appear to be reliable. The downside is that the R1100 is even heavier than the R100, at 243kg with a full tank of fuel. That's exacerbated by a high seat – it's actually adjustable for 860 or 840mm, but neither could be described as low. If you can live with its size though, there's much to recommend this first of the oilheads.

Slower selling, and slower on the road, was the R850 GS, offered between 1996 and 2001 with the smaller 848cc version of BMW's oil-cooled flat-twin. It weighs the same as its big brother, but power and torque figures are about the same as those of the R100, so performance is well down. It's even in the same insurance group as the R1100. However, being less sought after, it might be possible to pick up a bargain.

100%

R1150GS – 1998-2004
R1150GS Adventure – 2001-06

As BMW's entire line-up adopted the bigger 1130cc version of the oil-cooled flat-twin, so did the GS, the 1150 launched in 1998. It offered slightly more power and torque than the 1100, with 85bhp and 72lb/ft, thought this was offset by another weight increase to 249kg. Admittedly that was with a full tank of fuel, but this was the heaviest GS yet. The motorcycle press weren't impressed by that, or that the GS wasn't as quick as 100bhp machines, or that the gearchange still wasn't up to chain-drive standards. But everyone agreed

R1150 is heavier than the 1100, but offers more power and torque.

R1200 was very different to the 1150.

that despite its weight and size, the latest GS handled better than ever. The wide handlebars gave fine control and the bike had plenty of ground clearance, gaining a following among hard riders who found it as fast on twisty roads as many sports bikes.

The standard 1150 was joined in 2001 by the GS Adventure, capitalising on the fact that the GS was still the most capable adventure tourer off-road, even if most owners rarely ventured off tarmac. The changes were small, but included 20mm extra suspension travel, to 210mm front, 220mm rear, giving even more ground clearance and bump-swallowing ability than before. There was also progressive rear damping, a taller and wider screen, a bigger front mudguard, and crashbars to protect the fairing. One option was the Overland pack, which added a bigger 30-litre tank, knobbly tyres and, for picking ones way along boulder-strewn tracks, a lower first gear.

Opinions are mixed about the 1150 GS. It has all the same plus points as the 1100, making a superb long-distance tourer, as well as being very capable along twisty roads. And even if most owners wouldn't take it off-road, the bike certainly could do in the right hands. There's a very wide choice of 1150 GSs available secondhand, many of them with the expensive options of ABS and fitted luggage, but this was, and is, the heaviest GS ever, so it's not the easiest bike to manoeuvre. Although some have covered high mileage, others have been truly cosseted since new. There's little to recommend the Adventure, except for its rarity value, unless you really are planning on some serious off-road use.
R1150 GS: 150%
R1150 GS Adventure: 160%

R1200GS – 2004 on
R1200GS Adventure – 2006 on

The 1150 had been an update of the 1100, but in 2004 the R1200 GS was virtually a new bike. The oil-cooled flat-twin was redesigned with a balance shaft to smooth out some of the vibes, and offered more power than ever before – 100bhp and 85lb/ft. BMW also worked hard to take some weight out of the bike, and the 1200 was 30 kilos lighter than its predecessor, thanks to weight savings in just about every component. These included a new six-speed transmission, with a slicker gearchange than before, a single-wire CAN bus wiring loom and a lighter tubular steel frame. Braking was now BMW's EVO system, with integral ABS, the handlebar lever controlling both front and rear brakes. As before, the ABS could be switched off, and this allowed the brakes to be used separately, in the normal way. Recognising that the tall, heavy GS could be something of a handful for shorter riders, BMW offered low and high seat options in addition to the existing two-position seat, giving a total range of 810-890mm.

The Adventure added longer travel suspension and a bigger tank, amongst other things.

It was two years before a 1200 Adventure came along – in the meantime, the 1150 Adventure continued for hardcore travellers. Like this one, the 1200 Adventure added longer travel suspension to the basic bike, plus a beefier alternator, adjustable handlebars, 33-litre fuel tank, engine protection bars and extra-wide footrests.

R1200 GSs are sought after bikes that hold their value very well, despite selling in large numbers. That does mean there's a wide choice secondhand, so it shouldn't be difficult to find a good one. Anyone put off the 1100/1150 by their sheer size and weight will find the 1200 easier to get on with, as well as significantly faster, and just as comfortable.
R1200 GS: 200%
R1200GS Adventure: 210%

5 Before you view
– be well informed

To avoid a wasted journey, and the disappointment of finding that the bike does not meet your expectations, it will help if you're very clear about what questions you want to ask before you pick up the phone. Some of these points might appear basic, but when you're excited about the prospect of buying your dream bike, it's amazing how the most obvious things slip the mind ... Also, check the classified ads of bike magazines for current values of the model you are interested in.

Where is the bike?
Is it going to be worth travelling to the next county/state, or even across a border? A locally-advertised machine, although it may not sound very interesting, can add to your knowledge for very little effort, so make a visit – it might even be in better condition than expected.

Dealer or private sale?
Establish early on if the bike is being sold by its owner or by a trader. A private owner should have all the history, so don't be afraid to ask detailed questions. A dealer may have more limited knowledge of the bike's history, but should have some documentation. A dealer may offer a warranty/guarantee (ask for a printed copy).

Cost of collection and delivery?
A dealer may well be used to quoting for delivery. A private owner may agree to meet you halfway, but only agree to this after you have seen the bike at the vendor's address to validate the documents. Conversely, you could meet halfway and agree the sale, but insist on meeting at the vendor's address for the handover.

View – when and where?
It is always preferable to view at the vendor's home or business premises. In the case of a private sale, the bike's documentation should tally with the vendor's name and address. Arrange to view only in daylight, and avoid a wet day – the vendor may be reluctant to let you take a test ride if it's wet.

Reason for sale?
Do make it one of the first questions. Why is the bike being sold and how long has it been with the current owner? How many previous owners?

Condition?
Ask for an honest appraisal of the bike's condition. Ask specifically about some of the check items described in Chapter 6.

All original specification?
Many GSs have been modified over the years, but the accessories fitted tend to be top quality practical items: hard luggage, extra large fuel tank or heated grips. In view of that, the original spec is only really an issue if you're looking for an original 80 G/S or Paris Dakar.

Matching data/legal ownership?

Do frame, engine numbers and licence plate match the official registration document? Is the owner's name and address recorded in the official registration documents?

For those countries that require an annual test of roadworthiness, does the bike have a document showing it complies (an MoT certificate in the UK, which can be verified on 0845 600 5977)?

Does the vendor own the bike outright? Money might be owed to a finance company or bank: the bike could even be stolen. Several organisations will supply the data on ownership, based on the bike's licence plate number, for a fee. Such companies can often also tell you whether the bike has been 'written off' by an insurance company. In the UK these organisations can supply vehicle data:

HPI – 01722 422 422 – www.hpicheck.com
AA – 0870 600 0836 – www.theaa.com
RAC – 0870 533 3660 – www.rac.co.uk
Other countries will have similar organisations.

Insurance?

Check with your existing insurer before setting out – your current policy might not cover you if you do buy the bike and decide to ride it home.

How you can pay

A cheque/check will take several days to clear and the seller may prefer to sell to a cash buyer. However, a banker's draft (a cheque issued by a bank) is as good as cash, but safer, so contact your own bank and become familiar with the formalities that are necessary to obtain one.

Buying at auction?

If the intention is to buy at auction see Chapter 10 for further advice.

Professional vehicle check (mechanical examination)

There are often marque/model specialists who will undertake professional examination of a vehicle on your behalf. Owners clubs may be able to put you in touch with such specialists.

6 Inspection equipment

– these items will really help

This book
Before you rush out of the door, gather together a few items that will help as you work your way around the bike. This book is designed to be your guide at every step, so take it along and use the check boxes in Chapter 9 to help you assess each area of the bike you're interested in. Don't be afraid to let the seller see you using it.

Reading glasses (if you need them for close work)
Take your reading glasses if you need them to read documents and make close-up inspections.

Overalls
Be prepared to get dirty. Take along a pair of overalls, if you have them.

Digital camera
If you have the use of a digital camera, take it with you so that later you can study some areas of the bike more closely. Photograph any part of the bike that causes you concern.

A friend, preferably a knowledgeable enthusiast
Ideally, have a friend or knowledgeable enthusiast accompany you: a second opinion is always valuable.

Pen and paper
Detailed notes for yourself or to get mechanical estimates are always a good idea – especially if you are inspecting more than one bike before you decide on your purchase.

General condition

First impressions count. Does the bike look cared for, or neglected? Although the BMW GS has become the quintessential overland travellers' bike, very few of them are actually used to cross deserts and mountain ranges. But a minority of owners do like green-laning, so check the crashbars and bashplate for the inevitable scrapes and knocks that result. Check the crashbars (or the cylinder heads, if there are no crashbars), handlebar ends and footrests for signs that the bike has been dropped. Watch for shiny new parts on an otherwise faded bike. Knobbly off-road tyres, especially on airheads, are a sure sign that the owner ventures off-tarmac. This isn't necessarily a bad thing, but worth bearing in mind.

What's your general impression?
Superficially shiny or honest workhorse?

BMWs are well made, but their finish can suffer if neglected – steel bolt heads corrode, alloy furs up – if road salt isn't washed off regularly. And GSs often get used all year round, so winter roads are an issue. Such neglect doesn't always mean that the bike hasn't been looked after mechanically, but it'll certainly depress the price.

Engine/frame numbers

Check whether the engine and frame numbers tally with those on the documentation, which they must do if the bike is bona fide. Monolever airheads have the engine number stamped on the crankcase, just above the dipstick; on Paralevers, it's on the right-hand side of the crankcase. On both bikes, the frame number is found on the VIN plate just behind the headstock, and also stamped on the frame itself, just below the right-hand cylinder. As detailed later, some early Paralevers were mistakenly registered with the frame number as the engine number. On Monolevers, the engine and frame numbers should match. It's the same job with oilheads – check that the engine number, and the frame number on the VIN plate, correspond with those on the registration document.

Check that engine/frame numbers tally
with the documentation.

Documentation

If the seller claims to be the bike's owner, make sure he/she really is by checking the registration document, which in the UK is V5C. The person listed on the V5C isn't necessarily the legal owner, but their details should match those of whoever is selling the bike. Also use the V5C to check the engine/frame numbers.

An annual roadworthiness certificate – the MoT in the UK – is handy proof that the bike was roadworthy when tested, and a whole sheaf of them are evidence of the bike's history – when it was actively being used, and what the mileage was. The more of these come with the bike, the better.

Engine/rear end/suspension

Start the engine – it should turn over briskly and fire up straight away, and the oil and charge warning lights should go out once it's on a fast idle. Airhead twins should be mechanically quiet from cold, but expect to hear some valve noise from the top end as it warms up. This is normal, but do listen out for the rattle of a loose timing chain. Oilhead twins shouldn't rattle at all – if they do,

Oilhead twins should be mechanically quiet.

it's more likely to be due to an overdue service than any serious problem, though ask yourself why anyone would try selling a bike that needs servicing.

Switch off, and go round to the back of the bike, which should be on its centre stand. On all Paralever bikes (that's everything from 1988 on) check the rear pivot bearing by placing a hand over the joint between the driveshaft and final drive, then try rocking the rear wheel from side to side. If there's movement, the bearing needs replacing – if ignored, the U-joint could fail without warning. Now check the driveshaft splines for wear. With the bike in gear, rotate the wheel through its freeplay back and forth – there shouldn't be more than an inch or two of movement.

Paralever rear end – check that rear pivot bearing.

Visually check the front forks (airheads), front damper (oilheads) and rear shock (all bikes) for leaks. Sitting on the bike, push the front end down a few times, then bounce down on the seat. Does the suspension feel well damped, or floppy?

www.velocebooks.com / www.veloce.co.uk
All current books • New book news • Special offers • Gift vouchers

On Paralever bikes (all from 1988 on) check the swing arm pivot bearing and U-joint. They can fail without warning. The driveshaft splines should be well lubricated, so ask when this was last done.

Check front and rear shocks for leaks – many GSs cover big miles two-up with luggage, which is hard on the rear suspension. Shocks should be smooth and compliant, without bottoming out or bouncing.

Expect some valve noise from airheads when the engine's warm, but oilheads should be mechanically quiet – if they're not, it's more likely to be the result of an overdue service than terminal wear.

Damaged crashbars are signs that a bike has been dropped, or used enthusiastically off-road, or both. The same applies to the bashplate. GSs are designed to run off-road, but this inevitably takes its toll.

BMW alloy (of which there's plenty on the GS) will corrode if neglected and road salt isn't washed off. This is the result. It won't affect the running of the bike, but it can make it look tatty.

9 Serious evaluation

– 30 minutes for years of enjoyment

Circle the Excellent, Good, Average or Poor box of each section as you go along. The totting up procedure is detailed at the end of the chapter. Be realistic in your marking!

Engine/frame numbers

Ex Gd Av Po
4   3   2   1

The first job is to check whether the engine and frame numbers tally with those on the documentation. If they don't, make your excuses and walk away. On airheads the frame number is found on the VIN plate behind the headstock, and also stamped on the frame itself, just below the right-hand cylinder. The first seven digits of these two numbers should be the same. On Monolevers, the engine number is stamped on the crankcase, just above the dipstick. On Paralevers, it's on the right-hand side of the crankcase. Engine and frame numbers should match on the Monolevers, but early Paralevers had a different system, with non-matching numbers. This led to confusion among dealers, with some new bikes being registered with the frame number as the engine number. Five minutes work comparing the actual numbers with those on the registration documents should confirm whether

VIN plate is behind headstock.

the bike you're looking at is affected. If it is, it's not necessarily a sign of foul play. On oilheads, check that the engine number, and the number on the VIN plate, corresponds with that on the paperwork.

Frame number on airheads.

Check engine number corresponds with paperwork as well.

Paintwork is generally good quality, and lasts well.

Many bodywork parts are plastic.

Paint/alloy

BMWs are renowned for their quality finish, but don't let that lull you into a false sense of security – a GS neglected over the years will start to look tatty, just like any other bike. One thing you shouldn't need to worry about is chrome, as apart from the exhaust system there isn't any to speak of, and that on the exhaust is pretty good – in any case, many older bikes will have had downpipes, collector box or silencer, or all three, replaced by now.

Tank and panel paint finish lasts very well. On older bikes, expect it to be

Alloy will corrode if neglected.

faded and with the odd scratch, but that's hardly a serious problem. Airheads are more likely to have a tatty frame – again, it doesn't affect how the bike rides, but it's a good bargaining counter. If the frame has been powder coated, that's a good sign (of an owner prepared to put in time and money) so long as the coating was properly applied – if the metalwork isn't cleaned first, powder coating will eventually flake off.

There's lots of plain alloy on the GS – it looks good and can be wiped clean. But like any other alloy, it will corrode if not washed regularly. On oilheads, the bottom fork legs and rear hub are especially prone, and one R1150GS seen in research for this book had serious corrosion on the crankcase, with the protective coating bubbling up. GS alloy rims last well though, as do the spokes.

Bodywork

In one respect, buying a secondhand bike is far easier than purchasing a used car – there's far less bodywork to worry about. Crashbars to protect the cylinders are a popular option on all bikes, and make sure these aren't bent or scratched – if they are, quiz the owner as to how it happened. On the right-hand side of R100 airheads, the oil cooler is crashbar mounted, making it vulnerable to damage. Upper crashbars to protect the fuel tank and fairing are also well worth having. Also check the bashplate underneath the bike – damage here suggests that, unlike most GSs, the one you're looking at really has been used off-road. If the bashplate is scraped

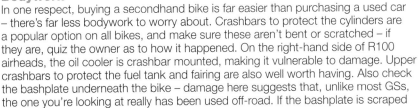

Plastic parts should be free of cracks and scuffs.

Big aftermarket tanks suggest high mileage trips.

and dented, ask the owner how the damage occurred. On the steel fuel tank (unless an aftermarket plastic one has been bolted on) check for signs of leakage along the seams, around the fuel tap and filler flap. Everything else – side panels, mudguards, headlight surround and (on R100GS Paris Dakar models) the fairing – is plastic. Check all of these for cracks, or paint flaking off, the former being evidence of a hard life, and possible off-road use. Cosmetic faults like these are another good bargaining counter, and it may be that the owner is one of those people who keeps the bike spot-on mechanically, but isn't too bothered about cosmetics. Some BMW owners are like that, especially if they cover a lot of miles, and that's not necessarily a bad thing. If you're looking to buy a tatty looking bike with a view to getting it back up to scratch, don't forget to factor in the time/money it'll take to do that.

If the bashplate has been scraped or dented, the bike will have been used off-road.

Badges/graphics

4 3 2 1

The GS was a departure for BMW in more ways than one. Not only was it the company's first production off-road bike, but it had a flamboyant character, breaking away from BMW's conservative touring image. To back that up, it had loud graphics on the tank – blue and red on the original Paris Dakars, the vertical '1000' in yellow on early black/yellow R100s, and so on. Check these for damage, as replacing them could be tricky on the older bikes. By contrast, oilhead GSs are almost graphic free and far more toned down, though their unique looks speak for themselves.

The badge that says it all for some.

It's not unknown for badge collectors to prize off BMW's blue and white roundel, so check the bike has two, one each side of the tank.

Original graphics like these may be hard to find, but they last well.

Seat ④ ③ ② ①

All GSs had a dual seat, apart the solo fitted to original Paris Dakars. You won't need to worry about rust, as they all had a fibreglass or plastic seat pan to save weight. As on any bike, the cover will split eventually, which of course allows rain in, which the foam padding soaks up – and once seat foam gets wet, it never dries out, giving you a permanently damp backside, or a rock hard seat on icy mornings. New covers and complete seats in various styles are available, though recovering an old seat is a specialist job.

All oilhead bikes have an adjustable seat, allowing a height of 840-860mm – check which setting the seat is on, and that you're comfortable with it. You should be able to get one foot comfortably flat on the ground. Unless you're a stickler for originality, there are plenty of good quality aftermarket seats around, and one of these shouldn't detract from the value of the bike. If seat height is a problem (even on the lower setting) then a seat specialist will cut it down and recover it for you.

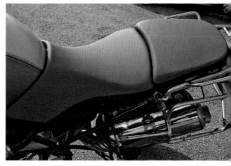

Oilhead GS seats come in two parts, for pilot and pillion.

Check seat for tears and splits.

Rubbers ④ ③ ② ①

On the airhead GSs, worn footrest rubbers are a sign of high mileage, though as they're so cheap and easy to replace, not an infallible one. They should be secure on the footrest and free of splits or tears. Oilhead 1100s and 1150s have alloy footrests with a small rubber pad, while 1200s have a serrated rest only – grippier for when you're slip-sliding along a tricky Saharan piste, or yomping through a quagmire track in the Congo. They also look quite cool outside the supermarket.

Worn footrest rubbers are a sure sign of high mileage.

R1200s have rubber-free serrated rests.

Frame

Ex 4 Co 3 Av 2 Po 1

The most important job on airheads is to check whether the main frame is straight and true. Crash damage may have bent it, putting the wheels out of line. One way of checking is with an experienced eye, string and a straight edge, but the surest way to ascertain a frame's straightness is on the test ride – any serious misalignment should be obvious in the way the bike handles.

Oilheads are completely different in that they don't have a conventional frame. Instead, everything is bolted, directly or indirectly, to the engine and transmission, which are the main stress bearing members of the entire bike. There is a rear subframe which supports the rear seat and rear light – remove the seat and check that this isn't broken or bent. Have a look at the main steering head casting for rippling or paint flaking off – signs of a heavy front end impact. If the Telelever front suspension doesn't work smoothly through its whole travel, that's more evidence that something is bent.

With crash damage in mind, have a look round the whole bike for clues. Minor scrapes on the cylinder heads could be just caused by enthusiastic riding, but anything more means the bike has been dropped. Are the crashbars damaged, or are they suspiciously new and shiny on an elderly bike, suggesting recent replacement? Ditto new mirrors, luggage rack and footrests. Are the handlebars straight and pointing in the right direction?

While looking at the crashbars on airheads, take a look at the bar-mounted oil cooler as well – if the crashbar has been damaged on that side, check that the cooler itself isn't damaged and that its mounts aren't twisted or cracked.

Finally, on the test ride, the bike should run straight and true when pointed down the road, without pulling to either side. It should go around corners without wobbles or weaves.

Signs of damage on this crashbar show that the bike has been dropped.

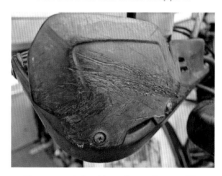

Even scratched handguards provide evidence of a spill.

Check the headstock on oilheads for signs of crash damage.

Stands

BMW GSs are heavy, but fortunately the centre stand is built to take it. As we've seen, leaving the bike on its side stand can lead to blue smoke from the left-hand cylinder on first starting up. In fact, the early airheads had no side stands as part of the deal – these were an option, mounted on the crashbars, and aftermarket stands were available which bolted to the frame. By now, most bikes will have been equipped with one, but airhead GS centre stands still got heavier use than on most bikes. The side stands that were factory-fitted can develop play, but they don't break.

The centre stand pivots wear eventually – when the bike is on the stand, try rocking it from side to side. On firm ground, it shouldn't move. The good news is that if the pivots are worn, it's only the stand that needs replacing – unlike some bikes, BMW

A side stand should work smoothly and be secure.

stands don't pivot directly through the crankcase. And even after years of use, they're unlikely to need replacing. The author has seen one stand with feet almost worn through, yet it was still perfectly strong and stable.

All oilheads had sidestands from the factory, and owners are more likely to use them for preference because the bikes are heavier. The same comments apply: stands should work smoothly (if they don't, that's a sign of lack of lubrication, and a neglectful owner) and the centre stand shouldn't allow the bike to move around on firm ground.

Centre stands are long-lasting. Check the bike doesn't move on the stand.

Wiring is complex, and fitting a new loom (even to a simpler, older bike) is time-consuming.

Electrics

BMW electrics are pretty reliable, but even on the early airheads – relatively simple bikes compared to an 1150 or 1200 oilhead – the wiring loom is a complex piece of kit. Complete new looms are available from BMW, even for the oldest bikes, though one of these will cost around ⬤x200. The multi-pin connectors will corrode over time, so a new loom is the ultimate answer, though there's a lot of labour involved in fitting one. When looking over the seller's bike, you can't really take off the tank

Check the operation of every electrical component, including the most obvious.

to check the state of the wiring, but you can check that absolutely everything electrical works as it should: lights, horn, indicators, all the warning lights and switchgear. If anything doesn't, that's a good downward lever on the price. With the bike on fast idle, the alternator light should go out. If it doesn't, the alternator isn't charging, and it tends to be the rotor that fails, rather than the stator– the good news here is that both are easy to get at under the front cover. All airheads have electronic ignition, and sometimes this can give up, but there's no warning – it either works, or it doesn't.

The comments about wiring loom, ancillaries and alternator also apply to the oilheads. If the starter is noisy on one of these later GSs, beware. If allowed to continue, it will eventually damage the teeth on the starter ring, and replacing that means separating the engine and gearbox – that involves a day's labour, and a hefty bill.

R1150s and 1200s use twinspark coils, which have been known to fail, sometimes both coils at the same time. Still, it's unlikely that anyone will attempt to sell a GS running on one pot. The earlier single-spark coils are more reliable.

One other electrical point to watch on oilheads is the battery – it's relatively small for the big job of turning two meaty pistons over compression. That's compounded by the extra electrical drain of the servo brakes on some 1200s.

Oilhead sensors to the supply engine management system can be vulnerable to weather.

You're unlikely to find electrical faults on a late model GS, but everything should still be checked.

Low mileage oilheads ideally have the battery on trickle charge while it's not being used, but as long as it starts the engine briskly from cold, there's nothing to worry about. Older non-sealed batteries should have the correct amount of electrolyte – anything less is a sign of neglect of this simple job – and while you're there, check for acid spills damaging the paintwork.

Wheels/tyres

Ex   Gd   Av   Po
④   ③   ②   ①

BMW are known for innovation, and on the GS even the wheels were forward thinking. They were conventional spoked alloy rims with tubed tyres on the first generation Monolever G/S, but the Paralever bikes went over to tubeless tyres. And how do you keep the air in on a spoked wheel with no tube? Simply run the spokes out to the side of the rim, beyond the tyre. Every GS since 1988 has used this patented system.

Whether the spokes run to the side or the centre of the rim, check that none

R100 GS front hub. Whichever bike you're buying, wheel bearings should be on the checklist.

If tyres have less than half the tread left, use that as a bargaining point.

are broken, bent or missing. This is unlikely to be a problem unless the bike has been used off-road, as the spokes are strong, good quality, big-gauge items. For that reason, they should all be in tension – to check, tap each one with a screwdriver blade, and a clear ring means they're nice and tight.

With the bike on its centre stand, spin each wheel. It should run true, and there should be no dents or dings in the rim – if there are, that's another sign the bike has been used off-road.

Now check the wheel bearings. These aren't expensive, but fitting them is a hassle, and if there's play it could affect the handling. To check them, put the bike on its centre stand, put the steering on full lock and try rocking the front wheel in a vertical plane, then spin the wheel and listen for rumbles. Do the same for the rear wheel.

Despite their size and weight, BMW GSs aren't especially heavy on tyres. The actual life depends on the rider – keen types who are heavy on the throttle and brakes, and/or do a lot of high speed, heavily laden motorway miles, will wear down that rubber far quicker than a more gentle rider. Ten- to fifteen-thousand miles per set isn't untypical for an airhead, which is pretty good for such a substantial machine.

The tyres should have a good 50% of their tread left – if they have less, factor in the replacement cost when bargaining over the price. Check them for damage and sidewall cracks. Look at the wear pattern: are they worn right round; or is the edge of the tread untouched by tarmac? The former suggests a hard rider (not necessarily a bad thing, so long as they've looked after the bike).

Tyre brand is often down to personal choice – Metzeler Tourance and Michelin T66 seem to suit the R1100GS, for example – but note that off-road or dual-purpose tyres don't have the ultimate grip of pure road tyres, and often wear out more quickly on tarmac. The 21in front wheel on airheads limits your choice of road tyres.

Steering head bearings

Like wheel bearings, steering head bearings don't cost an arm and a leg, but trouble here can affect the handling, and changing them is a big job. With the bike on the centre stand, swing the handlebars from lock to lock. They should move freely, with not a hint of roughness or stiff patches – if there is, budget for replacing the bearings. To check for play, put the steering on full lock, grip the base of the forks and try rocking them back and forth.

If there is movement at the fork clamp, then the steering head bearings are loose – they may just need adjusting, but they're just as likely to be dented and need replacing. It's easy to confuse movement here with play in the steering head bearings, the fork sliders themselves or (on oilheads) the Telelever pivot bearing. It might even be the centre stand wobbling! The bottom line is that movement of any sort here needs further investigation – whether you choose to bring in an expert, take the bike to a dealer or walk away from the whole deal is up to you. Or show the movement to the owner and use it as a bargaining tool. When testing the forks by pumping them up and down, a clonking sound or movement at the steering head again indicates that the bearings need attention.

Steering head bearings live here. They're not expensive items, but worn bearings will affect handling.

Front forks/Telelever

Ex Gd Av Po
[4] [3] [2] [1]

Let's start with the conventional telescopic forks of an airhead. With the bike on its centre stand, check for play in the forks by grasping the bottom of the legs and trying to rock the fork legs back and forth. As mentioned previously, if you do detect movement, the next step is to find out where it's coming from. You should be able to see movement in the forks, if that's where the wear is. On oilheads, it could be the Telelever balljoint that's worn – check this by placing a finger behind the balljoint while someone else rocks the forks.

The forks should also be parallel – that is, appear to be in the same plane when viewed from the side. If they're not, they may have been twisted after hitting something. Take the bike off the centre stand, front brake on and pump the forks up and down: they should move through their whole travel smoothly and freely with no squeaks or rattles.

Fork gaiters on airheads should be firmly in place and in good condition, with no tears. But even if they are, there's no guarantee that the fork seals aren't leaking. To check for this, grasp the gaiter and rub it against the fork tube: it should resist movement, but if it slides easily, the chances are that the fork leg is oily because the seal is leaking. Check both forks in this way – if one gaiter slides more easily than the other, you can be sure there's a problem.

Checking the single front shock of an oilhead is easier, as

Gaiters should be in place and free of tears.

The telescopic forks of an airhead should be checked for leaks and worn bushes.

33

On the Telelever front ends, this balljoint is a wear point.

there's no gaiter to hide it, so you can just make a visual check for leaks. If there are, then it'll need replacing. On the road test, anything that feels odd needs further investigation, though bear in mind that the Telelever has a different feel to conventional front forks, especially under braking – if you've never ridden one before, take a few minutes to acclimatise before passing judgement.

It looks tucked away, but the Telelever's single shock is easy to visually check for leaks.

Rear suspension

Ex   OK   Av   Po
 4   3   2   1

We're dealing with two different systems here – Monolever up to 1987, and Paralever (both air- and oilheads) from '88 on. In both cases, there's a single shock which should be checked for leaks in the usual way. To check the operation of the shock, sit on the bike and bounce up and down in the seat – the suspension should feel firm and compliant, and should stop bouncing when you do.

Check that the rear shock is damping efficiently, and isn't leaking ...

On the test ride, seek out the odd manhole cover or pothole – if the suspension feels oversoft and bouncy, then the rear shock may need replacing. Do make sure that the spring pre-load is adjusted properly for your weight though – on R1200s there's a handy remote control adjustment via a knob on the left-hand side of the bike.

... same goes for the oilhead rear shock, with its remote control adjustment.

Shaft/final drive

Ex   OK   Av   Po
 4   3   2   1

One great advantage of all BMW twins is their shaft drive, which makes chain adjustment and lubrication a thing of the past. However, they're not infallible. The Monolever rear end (1980-87) is a single-sided swing arm which contains the shaft, though like the conventional swing arm on earlier BMWs this was prone to lifting on acceleration and squatting on deceleration. The Paralever rear end fitted from 1988 sought to minimise this by adding a second U-joint just forward of the final drive, allowing the shaft to pivot in the swing arm tube. Meanwhile, a strut parallel to the

Paralever rear end works well, but check for excess movement at the rear wheel.

Check for play in the rear pivot bearing on Paralever rear ends.

tube (hence, 'Paralever') fed most of the drive forces back into the frame, rather than have them taken up by the shock.

It's a good system that cancels out 70% of the jacking effect, but the rear U-joint is more prone to failure, on both air- and oilheads. It doesn't help that the pivot bearing runs in the plastic cage, and it will need replacing every 30,000 miles or so. To check the pivot bearing and U-joint for wear, place a hand over the joint and try rocking the rear wheel from side to side. Any movement should be obvious. If the bike has been over-enthusiastically steam cleaned, water can seep down inside the swing arm tube, which doesn't do the bearings any good.

It's important to check for wear, because when the U-joints do give way, they do so without warning, and can lock the back wheel up in the process. On Paralever bikes, ask when the pivot bearing was last changed.

The rear wheel bolts directly to the hub on three studs (R80 G/S) or four (everything else). The driveshaft is on splines and these can wear, but only after fairly high mileage. There's normally a fair amount of backlash at the wheel due to a combination of the shaft splines and gearbox wear, which shows up in movement at the rim – one or two inches of movement is normal. On the test ride, listen for clunks from the rear end as you take up drive.

Rubber bellows should be tight and in good condition, to prevent water ingress.

Clutch

⁴ ³ ² ¹

Just like the tyres, clutch life depends on rider use and abuse, but oilheads should manage 50,000 miles before it's time for a new clutch plate, and airheads 60-70,000. Changing the plate takes two hours to complete on an airhead (that's for a competent BMW mechanic), so it's not a major job.

These are petrol stains – any sign of oil misting at the bellhousing on oilheads indicates a leaking rear crank oil seal.

The clutch shouldn't slip or drag – if it does slip the rear crankshaft oil seal may have given up, allowing oil onto the plate. The telltale sign here is a serious oil leak under the gearbox on airheads (oil collects in a depression just below the box) or an oil mist around the bellhousing joint on oilheads. Either way, the seal will have to be replaced, which on oilheads can mean a whole day's labour. Oilheads have an hydraulic clutch, and if the lever feels spongey, the most likely cause is a weeping slave cylinder.

On the test ride, if clutch take up is very sudden, with the bike lurching forwards, it's likely to be because the transmission input shaft splines haven't been lubricated, allowing the clutch plate to stick on dry splines. Again, ask the owner when the shaft was last greased. A few bikes had their transmissions poorly shimmed at the factory, which leads to similar symptoms, and if lubing the input shaft splines makes no difference, then that's the problem, though it's a rare one.

Check clutch master cylinder on oilheads for leaks.

Gearbox

If you've climbed straight off a modern Japanese motorcycle and onto a GS, especially an airhead, then be prepared for a culture shock. Thanks to the engine-speed clutch, mounted directly on the crankshaft, BMW gearchanges are slow and clunky compared to the best chain-driven bikes, though the later oilheads were a great improvement, and even the airhead GSs were better than BMWs of the 1970s.

In any case, although the change might be slow and (until you get the hang of it) clunky, it should be positive and engage all gears cleanly, with no missed shifts, false neutrals or jumping out of gear. Gear linkages on the airheads don't wear significantly, but the gearlever can partially seize in its bush on oilheads. With a very stiff gearchange, or the transmission stuck in one ratio, this seems a more serious problem than it is. The cause is simply that the gear lever bush gets sprayed by road grit and water, and heated by the nearby exhaust – replacement of the bush isn't a major job.

Airhead transmissions may rattle at idle when hot, but nine times out of ten

Gear linkage doesn't wear significantly on airheads, but don't expect a slick gearchange.

If the gearchange is stiff on oilheads, a partially seized lever could be the reason.

this is just normal wear – the noise should disappear when the clutch lever is pulled in. If it doesn't, there could be a more serious fault, and the gearbox bearings are a weak spot – they're positioned above the normal oil level and rely on splash lubrication.

BMW switchgear is idiosyncratic, but reliable.

Instruments/switchgear

4 3 2 1

Instruments should work smoothly, and the rev counter on every GS is electronic – the rev counter was an option on early G/Ss, but many had them fitted later on by dealers. If the speedometer isn't working, then a snapped cable is the most likely cause. The only issue with a secondhand bike is, how long hasn't the speedo been working for, and how many miles has the bike covered in the meantime?

R80/100 GSs had a simpler set-up – this one has been around the clock ...

There's a full range of instruments on oilheads, as on this 1150.

If there's one thing that gets motorcyclists exercised, it's BMW switchgear. Actually, this doesn't apply to the G/S, which has conventional switches, but the 1993-on bikes use BMW's idiosyncratic, multi-coloured set-up with no less than three indicator switches: left, right and cancel. BMW owners maintain that it's just a matter of getting used to them, especially the right thumb operated cancel switch, but they're worth bearing in mind on the test ride.

The good news is that this switchgear isn't particularly vulnerable to rain, and over-enthusiastic use of a jetwash can be remedied by a squirt of WD-40.

Cables

4 3 2 1

All the control cables – throttle, choke (if fitted), clutch – should work smoothly without stiffness or jerking. Early bikes have a cable-operated clutch and choke, but oilheads, with their hydraulic clutch and automatic

All cables should work smoothly, with outers in good condition.

choke, have just a throttle cable. Poorly lubricated, badly adjusted cables are an indication of general neglect, and the same goes for badly routed cables.

Engine – general impression

The good news is that by motorcycle standards the BMW flat-twin – airhead or oilhead – is very long lived. The bottom end is virtually unburstable, and there are plenty of bikes around with well over 100,000 miles showing on the original crank. Another testament to the engine's basic strength is the story of an R100 GS that was dropped at speed, hard enough to smash the cylinder and bend the con-rod on the side that went down, yet the crankshaft was fine.

One side of the engine of a brand new R1200 GS – it should be good for many years of service.

Usually, the only possible cause of crankshaft problems is a lack of oil, caused by a serious leak from the oil filter housing, but this is rare.

BMW's flat-twin – whether air- or oilhead – is a tough and long-lived motor.

That said, BMW twins need to be looked after, just like any other piece of engineering.

A tatty exterior appearance doesn't necessarily mean internal neglect, but watch out for chewed up fasteners where someone's tried to use the wrong size of Allen key. Ideally, the bike will have a full service history at a BMW franchise dealer or one of the well-known specialists, though that might be asking a bit much of a 25-year-old R80.

Engine – starting/running

On both air- and oilheads, the engine should turn over briskly and start straight away, settling down to a nice, even idle. Any vibration or lumpiness from low revs on an airhead indicates out of balance carburettors. Setting them up properly is a simple job for any experienced BMW mechanic, and certainly no reason to reject the bike out of hand. Incidentally, if your airhead does have a flat battery, then that's when the side-mounted kickstart comes into its own, though according to those who have used one, it's for emergencies only!

Oilheads are renowned for surging at low revs, though this can be minimised

The kickstart on airheads is for emergency use only!

by regular servicing. It's also worth checking the throttle spindle at the throttle body on each side. This runs straight into an alloy housing, which can wear, allowing play in the cable pulley, which upsets the engine management and lambda sensor, and thus the fuel settings. As well as uneven running, wear here is betrayed by a slight clattering from the spindle.

Engine – smoke/noise

Ex Gd Av Po

4 3 2 1

On start up, don't be alarmed by blue smoke from the exhaust – it's simply a BMW idiosyncracy, in that leaving the bike on its sidestand can allow oil to drain past the rings on the left-hand cylinder, which gets burnt off when the engine is next started. So long as the smoke disappears within a few minutes, all is well.

If the blue smoke doesn't go away, and especially if it appears on the overrun, then the most likely cause is worn valve guides – another relatively simple job for a

BMW mechanic. Airheads aren't known for high oil consumption, but they run best on mineral oil rather than synthetic. The bores are Nikasil lined, so the piston rings wear out first – another relatively simple and cheap job. The downside of Nikasil is that once it wears out, the cylinders can't be rebored, so you have to ditch the old barrels and buy new ones.

Oilhead twins – some use a lot of oil, some don't.

Like all air-cooled engines, airhead BMWs exhibit more mechanical noise than a water-cooled motor. So you should expect some valve gear rustle from the engine once it's warmed up, though it should be mechanically quiet from cold. The single-row timing chain will usually start to rattle from 15-20,000 miles onwards – these chains rarely break, but if left loose for too long will eventually flap around to damage the surrounding casing.

Don't be surprised to see blue smoke when first starting up – it could just be the result of oil drain into the left-hand cylinder.

Airhead twins will emit some valve rustle once warmed up.

R1200 twins should be mechanically quiet, even when hot.

Oilhead BMWs are often condemned for high oil consumption of one litre or more per 1000 miles, but it all depends – some do burn oil, some don't, and a lot seems to depend on the type of oil used, and the running-in procedure. Many riders use synthetic oil, thinking that it's the best, but with oil changes at 6000 miles it's not really necessary – plain 20/50 mineral oil, just like the airheads, is the official recommendation. Also, because synthetic oil is such an efficient lubricant, it prevents the engine bedding-in properly. The oilhead twin takes 12-24,000 miles to bed in, depending on use – harder riders will bed the engine in faster. Once nicely run in, and with mineral oil, it shouldn't burn a lot of oil.

The oilhead twin shouldn't be mechanically noisy, and if there's clatter from either head, the most likely cause is valve clearances and/or rocker end float, both of which should be checked and adjusted at service time. Although this is a relatively simple job, it does suggest that the bike hasn't been serviced for a while. Also listen for rattles from the camchain tensioner, though this very seldom gives trouble.

Oilhead BMWs do not leak oil – at least, not via drips, but an oil mist can appear around the bellhousing joint. This indicates crank or gearbox oil seal failure, which involves a relatively cheap component but a great deal of expensive labour. Also look for oil mist around the rear drive input seal.

Brakes

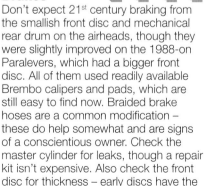

Don't expect 21st century braking from the smallish front disc and mechanical rear drum on the airheads, though they were slightly improved on the 1988-on Paralevers, which had a bigger front disc. All of them used readily available Brembo calipers and pads, which are still easy to find now. Braided brake hoses are a common modification – these do help somewhat and are signs of a conscientious owner. Check the master cylinder for leaks, though a repair kit isn't expensive. Also check the front disc for thickness – early discs have the

Airhead rear drum isn't a powerful stopper ...

minimum thickness stamped on. The original Monolever discs could wear in grooves thanks to dirt hiding in the drilled holes, but most bikes – they're all

... airhead front discs aren't super-powerful either.

at least 20 years old now – will have had replacement discs at some point. Even if the brakes are in tip-top condition, it's as well to remember that they don't give two-finger stopping, and ride accordingly.

With modern discs at both ends, the oilhead GSs from 1995 onwards are completely different, with strong braking from high speeds on demand. All the usual brake checks apply: fluid leaks from the master cylinder, pad thickness and the disc for thickness, scoring or a wear lip on the outer extremity. Also check that the bike rolls freely without the brakes dragging, as the 1200s and late 1150s are prone to sticking pads. The pad plates should always be coated with anti-seize compound whenever they're removed, and any competent owner or dealer will have done this.

Whatever the model, the brake fluid should be relatively clear and not cloudy, and the brake hoses should be free of cracks, kinks or leaks. Check how much life is left in the pads – once again, replacement isn't a big job, but it's another lever to bargain with.

On all bikes, check calipers for sticking pads, and brake pipe unions for leaks.

Things get complicated with the ABS fitted to 1150s and 1200s – if the warning light comes on, it may be something simple. For example, if the bike has been standing for a while and battery voltage is low, there may not be enough juice for the ABS to run though its self-check, so it'll disengage and the warning light will flash. A battery charge should have it back to normal. But if the ABS light stays on, then something more serious has gone wrong, which is a job for the BMW dealer. Don't go ahead with the purchase until you know what the fault is, and how much it'll cost to put right. Where fitted, the ABS system can be switched off, so if you don't trust such high-tech fitments, don't let its presence put you off.

R1200s have BMW's servo-assisted EVO braking system. If the electric servo failed (though there's no evidence that this happens), you would be left with 25% braking power, so it should be pretty obvious if something's wrong ... Once again, putting it right is a dealer job.

Master cylinders must be leak-free.

Exhaust

The first part of the GS exhaust system to succumb to rot isn't the downpipes or high-mounted silencer, but the collector box underneath the gearbox. In fact, the pipes and silencer last pretty well. Get down on the ground and poke the collector box with a screwdriver. If it does need replacing, then the ultimate answer is a complete stainless steel system, replacing the pipes, box and silencer in one go. The popular Keihan system can do away with the collector box altogether, using a Y-piece instead. If a previous owner has spent around ●x500 on a complete stainless steel system, that's a good sign of someone prepared to invest in the bike.

The downpipes and silencer last well.

The collector box is prone to rot.

Luggage

Despite their off-road pretensions, BMW GSs are often used as long distance tourers, and it's quite rare to come across one without some sort of hard luggage. Many GS riders do serious miles, and the accessories they buy tend to be of the practical kind – BMW's own heated grips, for example, are one such, and well worth having.

Although generic luggage, such as Givi, is available for the GS, most owners pay more for BMW's own factory luggage, the BMW-approved Touratech or the UK-made Metal Mule aluminium

Aluminium luggage often acts as a travelogue display board!

A topbox is a useful addition – check for signs of water ingress.

BMW in-house luggage will add to the bike's value.

The ultimate home-brewed luggage system, on Grant and Susan Johnson's much-travelled R80 GS.

panniers and top boxes. Whatever's fitted, don't be surprised to find that the left-hand pannier is smaller inside than the right – that's to make room for the upswept silencer, and all GSs suffer from it. Metal Mule does offer a tucked-in Scorpion exhaust which gets around the problem.

Whatever the make, check panniers for scuff marks, that the locks work smoothly and that there's no sign of water ingress. BMW, Touratech or Metal Mule luggage is good quality kit that will add to the value of the bike. Aluminium luggage is undeniably expensive, but bolsters the image of the GS as a two-wheeled Range Rover.

Test ride

Ex	Cd	Av	Po
4	3	2	1

However carefully you examine the bike and listen to the engine, there's no substitute for a test ride to get a real feel for what sort of condition it's in. This should be not less than 15 minutes, and you should be doing the riding – not the seller riding with you as pillion. It's understandable that some sellers are reluctant to let a complete stranger loose on their pride and joy, but it does go with the territory of selling a bike, and so long as you leave an article of faith (usually the vehicle you arrived in) then all should be happy. Take your driving licence in case the seller wants to see it.

The bike should start promptly, after which you should take time to familiarise yourself with the controls, tug at the levers and blip the throttle, to get a feel for the bike. Check that oil and ignition lights have gone out, select first gear (which should click in easily) and set off – clutch take-up should be smooth and progressive. Remember the advice previously about BMW gearchanges – don't expect super-slick shifting, but the change should be positive, with no false neutrals.

BMW twins don't have eye-popping power, but they do (all of them) have plenty of torque, so the test bike should accelerate briskly in all gears and respond instantly with no hiccups or hesitation. While accelerating, check the clutch isn't slipping. Shut down, and if the engine smokes on the overrun it's likely to need new valve guides. BMW GSs are not FireBlades, but the oilheads in particular handle very well indeed. The bike should turn in cleanly as soon as you nudge the bars, and be stable through any corner, with no wobbling. It should brake smoothly and progressively, whatever the model, though as noted above, airhead braking isn't up to modern standards.

Back at base, check that the engine settles back into a nice steady idle before switching off, and check for oil leaks when you climb off. If all's well, talk to the owner about price. If it isn't, and he won't make a deal, then thank him for his time and walk away.

Evaluation procedure
Add up the points scored
100 = first class, possibly concours; 75 = good/very good; 50 = average; 25 = poor.
Bikes scoring over 70 should be completely usable and require the minimum of repair, although continued maintenance and care will be required. Bikes scoring between 25 and 51 will require a full restoration – the cost of which will be much the same regardless of score. Bikes scoring between 52 and 69 will need very careful assessment of the repair/restoration costs so as to gain a realistic purchase value.

www.velocebooks.com / www.veloce.co.uk
All current books • New book news • Special offers • Gift vouchers

10 Auctions
– sold! Another way to buy your dream

Auction pros & cons
Pros: Prices will usually be lower than those of dealers or private sellers and you might grab a real bargain on the day. Auctioneers have usually established clear title with the seller. At the venue you can usually examine documentation relating to the bike.

Cons: You have to rely on a sketchy catalogue description of condition and history. The opportunity to inspect is limited and you cannot ride the bike. Auction machines can be a little below par and may require some work. It's easy to overbid. There will usually be a buyer's premium to pay in addition to the auction hammer price.

Which auction?
Auctions by established auctioneers are advertised in the motorcycle magazines and on the auction houses' websites. A catalogue, or a simple printed list of the lots for auctions might only be available a day or two ahead, though often lots are listed and pictured on auctioneers' websites much earlier. Contact the auction company to ask if previous auction selling prices are available as this is useful information (details of past sales are often available on websites).

Catalogue, entry fee and payment details
When you purchase the catalogue of the bikes in the auction, it often acts as a ticket allowing two people to attend the viewing days and the auction. Catalogue details tend to be comparatively brief, but will include information such as 'one owner from new, low mileage, full service history', etc. It will also usually show a guide price to give you some idea of what to expect to pay and will tell you what is charged as a 'buyer's premium'. The catalogue will also contain details of acceptable forms of payment. At the fall of the hammer an immediate deposit is usually required, the balance payable within 24 hours. If the plan is to pay by cash there may be a cash limit. Some auctions will accept payment by debit card. Sometimes credit or charge cards are acceptable, but will often incur an extra charge. A bank draft or bank transfer will have to be arranged in advance with your own bank as well as with the auction house. No bike will be released before all payments are cleared. If delays occur in payment transfers then storage costs can accrue.

Buyer's premium
A buyer's premium will be added to the hammer price: don't forget this in your calculations. It is not usual for there to be a further state tax or local tax on the purchase price and/or on the buyer's premium.

Viewing
In some instances it's possible to view on the day, or days before, as well as in the hours prior to, the auction. There are auction officials available who are willing to help out if need be. While the officials may start the engine for you, a test ride is out of the question. Crawling under and around the bike as much as you want is permitted. You can also ask to see any documentation available.

Bidding

Before you take part in the auction, decide your maximum bid - and stick to it!

It may take a while for the auctioneer to reach the lot you are interested in, so use that time to observe how other bidders behave. When it's the turn of your bike, attract the auctioneer's attention and make an early bid. The auctioneer will then look to you for a reaction every time another bid is made, usually the bids will be in fixed increments until the bidding slows, when smaller increments will often be accepted before the hammer falls. If you want to withdraw from the bidding, make sure the auctioneer understands your intentions – a vigorous shake of the head when he or she looks to you for the next bid should do the trick!

Assuming that you are the successful bidder, the auctioneer will note your card or paddle number, and from that moment on you will be responsible for the bike.

If it is unsold, either because it failed to reach the reserve or because there was little interest, it may be possible to negotiate with the owner, via the auctioneers, after the sale is over.

Successful bid

There are two more items to think about. How to get the bike home, and insurance. If you can't ride it, your own or a hired trailer is one way, another is to have it shipped using the facilities of a local company. The auction house will also have details of companies specialising in the transport of bikes.

Insurance for immediate cover can usually be purchased on site, but it may be more cost-effective to make arrangements with your own insurance company in advance, and then call to confirm the full details.

eBay & other online auctions

eBay and other online auctions could land you a GS at a bargain price, though you'd be foolhardy to bid without examining the bike first, something most vendors encourage. A useful feature of eBay is that the geographical location of the bike is shown, so you can narrow your choices to those within a realistic radius of home. Be prepared to be outbid in the last few moments of the auction. Remember, your bid is binding and that it will be very, very difficult to get restitution in the case of a crooked vendor fleecing you – caveat emptor!

Be aware that some bikes offered for sale in online auctions are 'ghost' machines. Don't part with any cash without being sure that the vehicle does actually exist and is as described (usually pre-bidding inspection is possible).

Auctioneers

Bonhams	www.bonhams.com
British Car Auctions BCA)	www.bca-europe.com
	or www.british-car-auctions.co.uk
Cheffins	www.cheffins.co.uk
eBay	www.ebay.com
H&H	www.classic-auctions.co.uk
Palmer Snell	www.palmersnell.co.uk
Shannons	www.shannons.com.au
Silver	www.silverauctions.com

11 Paperwork
– correct documentation is essential!

The paper trail
Ageing bikes sometimes come with a large portfolio of paperwork accumulated and passed on by a succession of proud owners. This documentation represents the real history of the machine, from which you can deduce how well it's been cared for, how much it's been used, which specialists have worked on it and the dates of major repairs and restorations. All of this information will be priceless to you as the new owner, so be very wary of bikes with little paperwork to support their claimed history.

Registration documents
All countries/states have some form of registration for private vehicles, whether its like the American 'pink slip' system or the British 'log book' system.

It is essential to check that the registration document is genuine, that it relates to the bike in question, and that all the details are correctly recorded, including frame and engine numbers (if these are shown). If you are buying from the previous owner, his or her name and address will be recorded in the document: this will not be the case if you are buying from a dealer.

In the UK the current (Euro-aligned) registration document is the V5C, and is printed in coloured sections of blue, green and pink. The blue section relates to the motorcycle specification, the green section has details of the registered keeper (who is not necessarily the legal owner), and the pink section is sent to the DVLA in the UK when the bike is sold. A small section in yellow deals with selling within the motor trade.

In the UK the DVLA will provide details of earlier keepers of the bike upon payment of a small fee, and much can be learned in this way.

If the bike has a foreign registration there may be expensive and time-consuming formalities to complete. Do you really want the hassle? Importing a bike from the USA for example involves a 6% import duty and 17.5% VAT as well as the cost of shipping and paperwork. It might be worthwhile if you're after a particularly rare bike (an early, original G/S for example, or a German-spec R65 GS) but there's such a wide choice of GSs in most European countries and the US, it's not really worth the hassle.

Roadworthiness certificate
Most country/state administrations require that bikes are regularly tested to prove that they are safe to use on the public highway. In the UK that test (the MoT) is carried out at approved testing stations, for a fee. In the USA the requirement varies, but most states insist on an emissions test every two years as a minimum, while the police are charged with pulling over unsafe-looking vehicles.

In the UK the test is required on an annual basis once a vehicle becomes three years old. Of particular relevance for older bikes is that the certificate issued includes the mileage reading recorded at the test date and, therefore, becomes an independent record of that machine's history. Ask the seller if previous certificates are available. Without an MoT the vehicle should be trailered to its new home, unless you insist that a valid MoT is part of the deal. (Not such a bad idea this, as at least you will know the bike was roadworthy on the day it was tested and you don't need to wait for the old certificate to expire before having the test done.)

Road licence
The administration of every country/state charges some kind of tax for the use of its road system, the actual form of the 'road licence' and how it is displayed varying enormously from country to country and state to state.

Whatever the form of the road licence, it must relate to the vehicle carrying it and must be present and valid if the bike is to be ridden on the public highway legally. The value of the licence will depend on the length of time it will continue to be valid.

In the UK if a bike is untaxed because it has not been used for a period of time, the owner has to inform the licencing authorities, otherwise the vehicle's date-related registration number will be lost and there will be a painful amount of paperwork to get it re-registered. Also in the UK, bikes built before the end of 1972 are road tax exempt, but this doesn't apply even to the oldest G/S.

Service history
Try to obtain as much service history and other paperwork pertaining to the bike as you can. Naturally specialist garage receipts score most points in the value stakes. However, anything helps in the great authenticity game, items like the original bill of sale, handbook, parts invoices and repair bills, adding to the story and the character of the machine. Even a brochure correct to the year of the bike's manufacture is a useful document and something that you could well have to search hard to locate in future years. If the seller claims that the bike has been restored, then expect receipts and other evidence from a specialist restorer.

If the seller claims to have carried out regular servicing, ask what work was completed, when, and seek some evidence of it being carried out. Your assessment of the bike's overall condition should tell you whether the seller's claims are genuine.

Restoration photographs
If the seller tells you that the bike has been restored, then expect to be shown a series of photographs taken while the restoration was under way. Pictures taken at various stages, and from various angles, should help you gauge the thoroughness of the work. If you buy the bike, ask if you can have all the photographs, as they form an important part of its history. It's surprising how many sellers are happy to part with their bike and accept your cash, but want to hang on to their photographs! In the latter event, you may be able to persuade the vendor to get a set of copies made.

12 What's it worth to you?

– let your head rule your heart!

Condition

If the bike you've been looking at is really ratty, then you've probably not bothered to use the marking system in chapter 9. You may not have even got as far as using that chapter at all!

If you did use the marking system, you'll know whether the bike is in Excellent (maybe concours), Good, Average or Poor condition or, perhaps, somewhere in between these categories.

To keep up to date with prices, buy the latest editions of the bike magazines (such as *Bike Trader* and *MCN* in the UK) and check the classified and dealer ads – these are particularly useful as they enable you to compare private and dealer prices. Most of the magazines run auction reports as well, which publish the actual selling prices, as do the auction house websites. Also check whether your national BMW club has a bikes for sale section – this may only be open to members, but if you're serious about buying a GS it'll be worth joining.

BMW GSs are relatively modern machines, and there are a lot of them around, so the usual rules about buying a classic bike as an investment don't apply, with the possible exception of a Paris Dakar. Airheads are still the cheapest bikes to buy, and the actual price reflects condition and mileage rather than age. Prices are unlikely to fall much further, and if anything interest in airhead GSs is stronger than ever, as they are seen as originators of the whole concept of an adventurer tourer.

Depreciation will affect the oilheads however, as they are newer machines in plentiful supply, and this situation is likely to continue for some time – at the time of writing, the GS remains BMW's most popular bike, selling in big numbers, with more coming onto the secondhand market all the time.

Before you start haggling with the seller, consider what affect any variation from standard specification might have on the bike's value. This is a personal thing: for some, absolute originality is non-negotiable, while others see non-standard parts as an opportunity to pick up a bargain. Do your research in the reference books, so that you know the bike's spec when it left the factory. That way, you shouldn't end up paying a top-dollar original price for a non-original bike.

If you are buying from a dealer, remember there will be a dealer's premium on the price.

Striking a deal

Negotiate on the basis of your condition assessment, mileage, and fault rectification cost. Also take into account the bike's specification. Be realistic about the value, but don't be completely intractable: a small compromise on the part of the vendor or buyer will often facilitate a deal at little real cost.

13 Do you really want to restore?

– it'll take longer and cost more than you think

There's a certain romance associated with restoration projects, restoring a sick bike back to blooming health, and it's tempting to buy something that 'just needs a few small jobs' to bring it up to scratch. But there are two things to think about: one, once you've got the bike home and start taking it apart, those few small jobs could turn into big ones. Two, restoration takes time, which is a precious thing in itself. Be honest with yourself – will you get as much pleasure from working on the bike as you will from riding it?

Of course, you could hand the whole lot over to a professional, and the biggest cost involved there is not the new parts, but the sheer labour involved. Such restorations don't come cheap, and in taking this route there are three other issues to bear in mind as well.

First, make it absolutely clear what you want doing. Do you want the bike to be 100% original at the end of the process, or simply useable? Do you want a concours finish, or are you prepared to put up with a few blemishes on the original parts?

Secondly, make sure that not only is a detailed estimate involved, but that it is more or less binding. There are too many stories of a person quoted one figure only to be presented with an invoice for a far larger one!

Third, check that the company you're dealing with has a good reputation – the owners club, or one of the reputable parts suppliers, should be able to make a few recommendations.

Restoring a BMW GS yourself requires a number of skills, which is fine if you already have them, but if you haven't it's good not to make your newly acquired bike part of the learning

Restoring a bike that's seen the world can be a big job.

Paying more for a well-kept GS could make more sense.

curve! Can you weld? Are you confident about building up an engine? Do you have a warm, well-lit garage with a solid workbench and a good selection of tools?

A rolling restoration is tempting, especially as the summer starts to pass with your bike still off the road. This is not the way to achieve a concours finish, which can only really be achieved via a thorough nut-and-bolt rebuild, without the bike getting wet, gritty and salty in the meantime. But there's a lot to be said for a rolling restoration. Riding the bike helps keep your interest up as its condition improves, and it's also more affordable than trying to do everything in one go. In the long run, it will take longer, but you'll get some on-road fun out of the bike in the meantime.

But maybe the bottom line is this. There are lots of BMW GSs around, many of them well cared for by knowledgeable owners. That also means that the GS isn't a collector's item (with the exception of early Paris Dakars), making a home restoration even less worthwhile. Better to buy a bike that's ready to ride, and enjoy it ...

With the big choice of GSs around, restoring a sick one doesn't make much sense, unless it's a real bargain.

Paint faults generally occur due to lack of protection/maintenance, or to poor preparation prior to a respray or touch-up. Some of the following conditions may be present in the bike you're looking at:

Orange peel
This appears as an uneven paint surface, similar to the appearance of the skin of an orange. The fault is caused by the failure of atomised paint droplets to flow into each other when they hit the surface. It's sometimes possible to rub out the effect with proprietary paint cutting/rubbing compound or very fine grades of abrasive paper. A respray may be necessary in severe cases. Consult a paint shop for advice.

Cracking
Severe cases are likely to have been caused by too heavy an application of paint (or filler beneath the paint). Also, insufficient stirring of the paint before application can lead to the components being improperly mixed, and cracking can result. Incompatibility with the paint already on the panel can have a similar effect. To rectify it is necessary to rub down to a smooth, sound finish before respraying the problem area.

Crazing shouldn't affect the original factory paint job.

Crazing
Sometimes the paint takes on a crazed rather than a cracked appearance when the problems mentioned under 'cracking' are present. This problem can also be caused by a reaction between the underlying surface and the paint. Paint removal and respraying the problem area is usually the only solution.

Blistering
Almost always caused by corrosion of the metal beneath the paint. Usually perforation will be found in the metal and the damage will usually be worse than

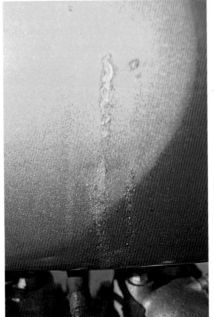

Blistering requires a respray.

that suggested by the area of blistering. The metal will have to be repaired before repainting.

Micro blistering
Usually the result of an economy respray where inadequate heating has allowed moisture to settle on the panel before spraying. Consult a paint specialist, but damaged paint will have to be removed before partial or full respraying. Can also be caused by bike covers that don't 'breathe.'

Fading
Some colours, especially reds, are prone to fading if subject to strong sunlight for long periods without the benefit of polish protection. Sometimes proprietary paint restorers and/or paint cutting/rubbing compounds will retrieve the situation. Often a respray is the only real solution.

Peeling
Often a problem with metallic paintwork when the sealing lacquer becomes damaged and begins to peel off. Poorly applied paint may also peel. The remedy is to strip and start again.

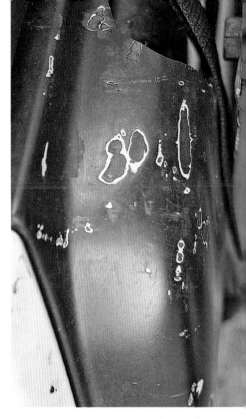

Colour finish wears off plastic, which then needs repainting.

Dimples
Dimples in the paintwork are caused by the residue of polish (particularly silicone types) not being removed properly before respraying. Paint removal and repainting is the only solution.

15 Problems due to lack of use
– just like their owners, GSs need exercise!

Like any piece of engineering, and indeed like human beings, BMW GSs deteriorate if they sit doing nothing for long periods. This is especially relevant if the bike is laid up for six months of the year, as some machines are.

Rust attacks damp metal.

Rust
If the bike is put away wet, and/or stored a cold, damp garage, the paint, metal and brightwork will suffer. Ensure the machine is completely dry and clean before going into storage, and if you can afford it, invest in a dehumidifier to keep the garage atmosphere dry.

Seized components
Pistons in brake calipers can seize partially or fully, resulting in binding or non-working brakes. Cables are vulnerable to seizure too – the answer is to thoroughly lube them beforehand, and come into the garage to give them a couple of pulls once a week or so.

Lack of use can result in sticking pads and dragging brakes.

Tyres
If the bike's been left on its side stand, most of its weight is on the tyres, which will develop flat spots and cracks over time. Always leave the bike on its centre stand, which takes weight off the tyres.

Engine
Old, acidic oil can corrode bearings. Many riders change the oil in the spring, when they're putting the bike back on the road, but really it should be changed just before the bike is laid up, so that the bearings are sitting in fresh oil. The same goes for the gearbox. While you're giving the cables their weekly exercise, turn the engine over slowly on the kickstart (if there is one), ignition off. Don't start it though – running the engine for a short time does more harm than good, as it produces a lot of moisture internally, which the engine doesn't get hot enough to burn off. This moisture will attack the engine internals, and the silencers.

If the bike's been standing, when was the oil last changed? Is it at the correct level?

Battery/electrics
Either remove the battery and give it a top-up charge every couple of weeks, or connect it up to a battery top-up device such as the Optimate, which will keep it permanently fully charged. Damp conditions will allow fuses and earth connections to corrode, storing up electrical troubles for the spring. Eventually, wiring insulation will harden and fail.

16 The Community
– key people, organisations and companies in the GS world

Auctioneers
See Chapter 10

Useful websites
BMW Official Website (Germany)
www.bmw-motorrad.com
See national websites (www.bmw-motorrad.co.uk for UK) for BMW dealer listings.

R1200 GS
www.bmwr1200gs.com
– lots of detailed info on the 1200 GS

BMW Information
www.bmbikes.co.uk
– excellent information site on all BMWs

Clubs across the world
Australia
BMW Club Australia
www.clubs.bmw.com.au

Austria
BMW Clubs Osterreich
www.bmw-club-europa.org

Belgium
BMW Club Vlaanderen
www.bmw-mc-vl.be

France
BMW Moto Club
www.bmwmcf.com

Germany
BMW Club Deutschland eV
www.bmw-club-deutschland.de

Greece
BMW Riders club of Greece
www.bmwriders.gr

The Netherlands
GS Club
www.bmwgsclub.nl

Norway
BMW Klubben Norge
www.bmw.mc.no

Poland
BMW Klub
www.bmw-klub.pl

South Africa
BMW MC Club Pretoria
www.bmwclubs.co.za

Sweden
BMW MC Klubben
www.bmw-mc-klubben.se

UK
BM Riders Club
www.bmridersclub.com
01299 878507

BMW Owners Club
www.bmw-club.org.uk
0800 084 4045

GS Club
www.gsclubuk.org

UKGSer
www.ukgser.com

Airheads Beemer Club
www.airheads.org

USA
BMW Motorcycle Owners of America
www.bmwmoa.org

UK BMW specialists
All provide a servicing/repair service, unless otherwise stated. For your nearest official BMW dealer, go to the national official BMW website.

Motobins – spares
www.motobins.co.uk
01775 680881

Motorworks – spares
www.motorworks.co.uk
0845 458 0077

Dorset
CW Motorcycles
01305 269370
www.cwmotorcycles.co.uk

Glasgow
Bikerite Motorcycle Sales
0141 643 2200

Leicester
The Boxer Man
– servicing, repairs, restoration
www.boxerman.co.uk
0116 266 8913

Lincolnshire
Scriminger Engine Developments
01529 300434
email: scriminger@btinternet.co.uk

London
Bob Porecha
0208 659 8860
email: bob@porecha.fslife.co.uk

Hughes Motorcycles
0208 669 1706

Kinglake Motorcycles
0207 266 1378

Norwich
KRF Motorcycles
01603 629916

Oxfordshire
Premier Bikes
01235 519195

Redcar & Cleveland
D. Metcalf
01287 635274

Books
BMW Twins: The Complete Story
– Mick Walker, Crowood Press

BMW Motorcycle Buyers Guide
– Mark Zimmerman & Brian J Nelson, Motorbooks

The BMW Story – Ian Falloon, Haynes Publishing

How to Restore Your BMW Twin 1955-85 – Mick Walker, Motorbooks

BMW Motorcycles: The Complete Story
– Bruce Preston, Crowood Press

BMW 2-valve Twins 1970-96 Service Manual – Haynes Publishing

BMW 850, 1100 & 1150 1993-2003 Service Manual – Haynes Publishing

17 Vital statistics
– essential data at your fingertips

To list the specification of every BMW GS variant would take up more room than we have here, so here are three representative bikes: 1980 R80 G/S, 1993 R1100 GS and 2006 R1200 GS Adventure.

Engine
1980 R80 G/S: Air-cooled twin-cylinder horizontally opposed, ohv, bore x stroke 84.8 x 70.6mm, capacity 797cc, compression ratio 8.2:1, max power 50bhp @ 6500rpm, max torque 41lb/ft @5000rpm
1993 R1100 GS: Oil-cooled twin-cylinder horizontally opposed, high cam, bore x stroke 99 x 70.5mm, capacity 1085cc, compression ratio 10.3:1, max power 80bhp @ 6750rpm, max torque 71lb/ft @ 5250rpm
2006 R1200 GS Adventure: Oil-cooled twin-cylinder horizontally opposed, high cam, bore x stroke 101 x 73mm, capacity 1170cc, compression ratio 11.0:1, max power 100bhp @ 7000rpm, max torque 85lb/ft @ 5500rpm

Gearbox
1980 R80 G/S: 5-speed, ratios 4.4, 2.86, 1.67, 1.50:1
1993 R1100 GS: 5-speed, ratios 4.16, 2.91, 2.13, 1.74, 1.45:1
2006 R1200 GS Adventure: 6-speed, ratios 2.277, 1.583, 1.259, 1.033, 0.903, 0.805:1

Brakes
1980 R80 G/S: Front 260mm disc, 2-pot caliper, rear 200mm drum
1993 R1100 GS: Front twin 305mm discs, 4-pot calipers, rear 276mm disc
2006 R1200 GS Adventure: EVO integral ABS, Front twin 305mm discs, 4-pot calipers, rear 265mm disc

Electrics
1980 R80 G/S: 12v, 280w alternator
1993 R1100 GS: 12v, 700w alternator
2006 R1200 GS Adventure: 12v 720w three-phase alternator

Dimensions
1980 R80 G/S: 2230 x 820 x 1150mm
1993 R1100 GS: 2189 x 920 x 1366mm
2006 R1200 GS Adventure: 2250 x 955 x 1470mm

Wheelbase
1980 R80 G/S: 1465mm
1993 R1100 GS: 1509mm
2006 R1200 GS Adventure: 1510mm

Seat height
1980 R80 G/S: 860mm

1993 R1100 GS: 840/860mm
2006 R1200 GS Adventure: 890/910mm

Weight (with full tank of fuel)
1980 R80 G/S: 186kg
1993 R1100 GS: 243kg
2006 R1200 GS Adventure: 223kg (dry)

Max speed
1980 R80 G/S: 104mph
1993 R1100 GS: 121mph
2006 R1200 GS Adventure: over 124mph

Model changes by year
1980: R80 G/S launched
1981: Hubert Auriol wins Paris-Dakar Rally on a G/S
1982: R80 ST launched
1984: R80 G/S Paris Dakar launched
1985: R80 ST dropped
1988: Second generation R80 and R100 GS replace R80 G/S
1990: R100 GS Paris Dakar launched
1993: R1100 GS launched
1994: R100 Paris Dakar dropped
1996: R80 GS Basic (one year only) & R850 GS launched
1997: R80 GS Kalahari (one year only)
1998: R1150 GS replaces R1100 GS
2001: R1150 GS Adventure launched
2004: R1200 GS replaces R1150 GS – 1150 Adventure continues
2006: R1200 GS Adventure replaces 1150 Adventure

£9.99-£12.99 / $19.95
(prices subject to change, p&p extra).

For more details visit
www.veloce.co.uk
or email info@veloce.co.uk

Also from Veloce Publishing ...

ISBN: 978-1-845843-25-0
Hardback • 25x25cm
• £19.99* UK/$39.95* USA
• 128 pages • 270 colour
and b&w pictures

BMW Custom Motorcycles

Choppers, Cruisers, Bobbers, Trikes & Quads
Uli Cloesen

Customising BMWs – does it work? This book, the first of its kind solely devoted to the BMW custom bike scene, proves that it does! Features stunning images of customised BMW singles, twins and fours from contributors around the globe, many complemented by owners' stories and technical descriptions.

ISBN: 978-1-845845-29-2
Hardback • 25x25cm
• £25* UK/$39.95* USA
• 128 pages • 205 colour
pictures

BMW Café Racers
Uli Cloesen

Showcasing fantastic custom BMW café racers from all over the globe, from the old to the new, this book presents them in all their innovative glory. Featuring owner's stories and technical descriptions, BMW Café Racers is a book guaranteed to interest BMW fans and members of the café racer scene alike – see the 'caféd' side of BMW.

*prices subject to change, p&p extra.
For more details visit www.veloce.co.uk or email info@veloce.co.uk

Index